Book 1
Windows 8 Tips for Beginners
BY SAM KEY

&

Book 2
PHP Programming
Professional Made Easy
BY SAM KEY

Book 1
Windows 8 Tips for Beginners
BY SAM KEY

A Simple, Easy, and Efficient Guide to a Complex System of Windows 8!

Programming Box Set #97: Windows 8 Tips for Beginners & PHP Programming Professional Made Easy

Programming Box Set #97: Windows 8 Tips for Beginners & PHP Programming Professional Made Easy

Table Of Contents

Introduction

I want to thank you and congratulate you for purchasing the book, "Windows 8 Tips for Beginners: A Simple, easy, and efficient guide to a complex system of windows 8!"

This book contains proven steps and strategies on how to familiarize yourself with the new features of Windows 8 which were designed to make your computing experience simpler and more enjoyable. You will not only learn how to navigate through Windows 8 , but you will also learn how Windows 8 is similar to and different from the older versions so you can easily adjust and take advantage of the benefits that Windows 8 has in store for you.

Thanks again for purchasing this book, I hope you enjoy it!

Chapter 1: How is Windows 8 Different from Previous Versions?

With Windows 8, Microsoft launched a lot of new changes and features, some of which are minor , but others are major. Some of the changes you can see in Windows 8 are the redesigned interface, enhanced security and other online features.

Changes in the Interface

The most glaring change you will observe when you first open your computer with Windows 8 is that the screen looks completely different from older Windows versions. The Windows 8 interface has new features such as Start screen, hot corners, and live tiles.

•   The Start screen will be the main screen where you will find all of your installed programs and they will be in the form of "tiles". You can personalize your Start Screen by rearranging the tiles, selecting a background image and changing the color scheme.

•   You can navigate through Windows 8 using the "hot corners", which you activate by hovering the mouse pointer over the corners of the screen. For instance, if you want to switch to another open application, hover your mouse in the top-left corner of your screen and then click on the app.

•   Certain apps have Live Tile functions, which enable you to see information even if the app itself is not open. For instance, you can easily see the current weather on the Weather app tile from your Start screen; if you want to see more information, you can just click on the app to open it.

•   You can now find many of the settings of your computer in the Charms bar that you can open by hovering the mouse in the bottom-right or top-right corner of your computer screen.

Online Features in Windows 8

**Programming Box Set #97: Windows 8 Tips for Beginners & PHP
Programming Professional Made Easy**

Because of the ease of accessing Internet now, many people have started to save their documents and other data online. Microsoft has made it easier to save on the cloud through their OneDrive service (this was formerly called SkyDrive). Windows 8 is capable of linking to OneDrive and other online social networks such as Twitter and Facebook in a seamless manner.

To connect your computer to OneDrive, sign in using your free Microsoft account instead of your own computer account. When you do this, all of the contacts, files and other information stored in your OneDrive are all in your Start screen. You can also use another computer to sign in to your Microsoft account and access all of your OneDrive files. You can also easily link your Flickr, Twitter and Facebook accounts to Windows 8 so you will be able to see the updates straight from your Start screen. You can also do this through the People app which is included in Windows 8.

Other Features

•   The Desktop is now simpler for enhanced speed. Yes, the Desktop is still included in Windows 8 and you can still manage your documents or open your installed programs through the Desktop. However, with Windows 8, a number of the transparency effects that frequently caused Windows Vista and Windows 7 to slow down are now gone. This allows the Desktop to operate smoother on nearly all computers.

•   The Start menu, once considered as a vital feature in previous Windows versions, is now the Start screen. You can now open your installed programs or search for your files through the Start screen. This can be quite disorienting if you are just starting with Windows 8.

•   Windows 8 has enhanced security because of its integrated antivirus program referred to as Windows Defender. This antivirus program is also useful in protecting you from different kinds of malware. In addition, it can aid in keeping you and your computer secure by telling you which data each of your installed apps can access. For instance, certain apps can access your location, so if you do not want other people to know where you are, just change your preference in the settings/configuration part of your apps.

How to Use Windows 8

Because Windows 8 is not like the older versions, it will possibly change how you have been using your computer. You may need quite some time to get accustomed to the new features, but you just need to remember that those changes are necessary to enhance your computing experience. For instance, if you have used older Windows versions, you may be used to clicking on the Start button to launch programs. You need to get used to using the Start screen with Windows 8. Of course, you can still use the Desktop view to make file and folder organization easier and to launch older programs.

You may need to switch between the Desktop view and the Start screen to work on your computer. Don't feel bad if you feel disoriented at first because you will get used to it. Moreover, if you just use your computer to surf the internet, you may be spending majority of your time in the Start screen anyway.

Chapter 2: How to Get Started with Windows 8

Windows 8 can truly be bewildering at the start because of the many changes done to the interface. You will need to learn effective navigation of both the Start screen and Desktop view. Even though the Desktop view appears similar to the older Windows versions, it has one major change that you need to get used to – the Start menu is no more.

In this chapter, you will learn how to work with the apps and effectively navigate Windows 8 using the Charms bar. You will learn where to look for the features that you could previously find in the Start menu.

How to Sign In

While setting up Windows 8, you will be required to create your own account name and password that you will use to sign in. You can also opt to create other account names and associate each account name with a specific Microsoft account. You will then see your own user account name and photo (if you have uploaded one). Key in your password and press enter. To select another user, click on the back arrow to choose from the available options. After you have signed in, the Start screen will be displayed.

How to Navigate Windows 8

You can use the following ways to navigate your way through Windows 8

•   You can use the hot corners to navigate through Windows 8. You can use them whether you are in the Desktop view or in the Start screen. Simply hover your mouse in the corner of the screen to access the hot corners. You will see a tile or a toolbar that you can then click to open. All the corners perform various tasks. For instance, hovering the pointer on the lower-left corner will return you to the Start screen. The upper-left corner will allow you to switch to the last application that you were using. The lower-right or upper-right corners gives you access to the Charms bar where you can either manage your printers or adjust the settings of your computer. Hover your mouse towards the upper-left corner and then move your mouse down to see the list of the different applications that you are simultaneously using. You can simply on any application to go back to it.

• You can also navigate through Windows 8 through different keyboard shortcuts.

    o Alt+Tab is the most useful shortcut; you use it to switch between open applications in both the Start screen and Desktop view.

    o You can use the Windows key to go back to the Start screen. It also works in both the Desktop view and Start screen.

    o From the Start screen, you can go to the Desktop view by clicking on Windows+D.

• You can access the settings and other features of your computer through the toolbar referred to as Charms bar. Place your mouse pointer on the bottom-right or top-right corner of your screen to display the Charms bar wherein you can see the following icons or "charms":

    o The Search charm allows you to look for files, apps or settings on your computer. However, a simpler method to do a search is through the Start screen wherein you can simply key in the name of the application or file that you want to find.

    o You can think of the Share charm as a "copy and paste" attribute that is included in Windows 8 to make it easier for you to work with your computer. Using the Share charm, you can "copy" data like a web address or a picture from one app and then "paste" it onto another application. For instance, if you are reading a certain article in the Internet, you can share the website address in your Mail application so you can send it to a friend.

    o The Start charm will allow you to go back to the Start screen. If you are currently on the Start screen, the Start charm will launch the latest app that you used.

o The Devices charm displays all of the hardware devices that are linked to your computer such as monitors and printers.

o Through the Settings charm, you can open both the general setting of your computer and the settings of the application that you are presently using. For instance, if you are presently using the web browser, you can access the Internet Options through the Settings charm.

How to Work with the Start Screen Applications

You may need to familiarize yourself with the Start screen applications because they are quite different from the "classic" Windows applications from previous versions. The apps in Windows 8 fill the whole screen rather than launching in a window. However, you can still do multi-tasking by launching two or more applications next to each other.

• To open an application from the Start screen, look for the app that you want to launch and click on it.

• To close an application hover your mouse at the top portion of the application, and you will notice that the cursor will become a hand icon, click and hold your mouse and then drag it towards the bottommost part of the screen and then release. When the app has closed, you will go back to the Start screen.

How to View Apps Side by Side

Even though the applications normally fill up the whole screen, Windows 8 still allows you to snap an application to the right or left side and then launch other applications beside it. For instance, you can work on a word document while viewing the calendar app. Here are the steps to view applications side by side:

1. Go to the Start screen and then click on the first app that you want to open.

2. Once the app is open, click on the title bar and drag the window to the left or right side of your computer screen.

3.   Release your mouse and you will see that the application has snapped to the side of your computer screen.

4.   You can go back to the Start screen by clicking at any empty space of the computer screen.

5.   Click on another application that you want to open.

6.   You will now see the applications displayed side by side. You can also adjust the size of the applications by dragging the bar.

Please note that the snapping feature is intended to work with a widescreen monitor. Your minimum screen resolution should be 1366 x 768 pixels to enjoy the snapping feature fully. If your monitor has a bigger screen, you will be able to snap more than two apps simultaneously.

How to cope with the Start menu

Many people have already complained about the missing Start menu in Windows 8. For many Windows users, the Start menu is a very vital feature because they use to open applications, look for files, launch the Control Panel and shut down their computer. You can actually do all of these things in Windows 8 too, but you will now have to look for them in different locations.

•   There are a number of ways to launch an application in Windows 8. You can launch an app by clicking the application icon on the taskbar or double-clicking the application shortcut form the Desktop view or clicking the application tile in the Start screen.

•   You can look for an app or a file by pressing the Windows key to go back to the Start screen. When you are there, you can simply key in the filename or app name that you want to look for. The results of your search will be immediately displayed underneath the search bar. You will also see a list of recommended web searches underneath the search results.

•   You can launch the Control Panel by going to the Desktop view and then hovering your mouse in the lower-right corner of the computer screen to display the Charms bar and then selecting Settings. From the Settings Pane, look for and choose Control Panel.

After the Control Panel pops up, you can start choosing your preferred settings.

•   You can shut down your computer by hovering the mouse in the lower-right corner of your screen to display the Charms bar and then selecting Settings. Click on the Power icon and then choose Shut Down.

Start Screen Options

If you prefer to continue working with the Desktop view more often, you actually have a number of alternatives that can let your computer operate more like the older Windows versions. One of these alternatives is the "boot your computer directly to the Desktop" rather than the Start screen. Here are the steps to change your Start screen options:

1.   Return to the Desktop view.

2.   Right-click the taskbar then choose Properties.

3.   You will then see a dialog box where you can choose the options that you want to change.

Chapter 3: How to Personalize Your Start Screen

If you are open to the idea of spending most of your time on the Start screen of your computer, there are different ways you can do to personalize it based on your preferences. You can change the background color and image, rearrange the applications, pin applications and create application groups.

• You can change the background of your Start screen by hovering the mouse in the lower-right corner of your screen to open up the Charms bar and then selecting the Settings icon. Choose Personalize and then choose your preferred color scheme and background image.

• You can change the lock screen picture by displaying the Charms bar again and the selecting the Settings icon. Choose Change PC settings and then choose Lock screen that is located near to the topmost part of the screen. Choose your preferred image from the thumbnail photos shown. You can also opt to click on Browse to choose your own photos. You will see the lock screen every time you return to your computer after leaving it inactive for a set number of minutes. However, you can also manually lock your screen by clicking on your account name and then choosing Lock.

• You can change your own account photo by displaying the Charms bar and then choosing the Settings icon. Click on the Change PC setting and choose Account picture. You can look for your own photos by clicking Browse, will let you browse the folders in your computer. Once you find the picture you want to use, click on Choose image to set it as your account picture. If you are running a laptop, you can also use the built-in webcam to take a picture of yourself for your account photo.

How to Customize the Start Screen Applications

You do not really need to put up with the pre-arranged apps on your Start screen. You can change how they look by rearranging them based on your own preference. You can move an app by clicking, holding and dragging the application to your preferred location. Let go of your mouse and the app tile will automatically move to the new place.

You may also think that the animation in the live tiles is very disturbing while you are working. Do not worry because you can simply turn the animation off so that you will only see a plain background. You can do this by right-clicking the application that you wish to change. A toolbar pop up from the bottom part of your computer screen. Simply choose Turn live tile off and the animation if you don't want real-time notifications.

How to Pin Applications to the Start Screen

By default, you won't be able to see all of the installed applications on the Start screen. However, you can easily "pin" your favorite apps on the Start screen so you can access them easily. You can do this by clicking the arrow found in the bottom-left corner of your Start screen. You will then see the list of all the applications that you have installed. Look for the app you want to pin and the right-click it. You will see Pin to Start at the lowest part of the screen. Click on it to pin your app.

To unpin or remove an application from the Start screen, right-click the app icon you want to remove and then choose "Unpin from Start".

How to Create Application Groups

There are more ways to bring organization to your apps. One way is to create an app group wherein you can similar apps together. You can give a specific name for each app group for easier retrieval. You can create a new application group by clicking, holding and dragging an application to the right side until you see it on an empty space of the Start screen. Let go of your mouse to let the app be inside its own application group. You will be able to see a distinct space between the new app group that you have just created and the other app groups. You can then drag other apps into the new group.

**Programming Box Set #97: Windows 8 Tips for Beginners & PHP
Programming Professional Made Easy**

You can name your new application group by right clicking any of the apps on the Start screen and then clicking Name group at the top of the application group. When choosing a group name, opt for shorter, but more descriptive names. After you have keyed in your group name, press the Enter key.

Chapter 4: How to Manage Your Files and Folders

The File Explorer found in the Desktop view is very handy in managing files and folders in your computer. If you are familiar with older Windows version, File Explorer is actually the same as Windows Explorer. You will usually use the File Explorer for opening, accessing and rearranging folders and files in the Desktop view. You can launch the File Explorer by clicking the folder icon found on the taskbar.

The View tab in the File Explorer enables you to alter how the files appear inside the folders. For instance, you may choose to the List view when viewing documents and the Large Icons view when looking at photos. You can change the content view by selecting the View tab and then choosing your preferred view from the Layout group.

For certain folders, you can also sort your files in different ways – by name, size, file type, date modified, date created, among others. You can sort your files by selecting the View tab, clicking on the Sort by button and then choosing your preferred view from the drop-down list.

How to Search Using the File Explorer

Aside from using the Charms bar to look for files, you can also use the Search bar in the File Explorer. Actually, the File Explorer provides search options that are more advanced than those offered by the Charms bar. This is very useful when you are finding it quite hard to look for a particular document.

Every time you key in a word into the search bar, you will see that the Search Tools tab automatically opens on the Ribbon. You can find the advanced search options on the Search Tools tab. You can use them to filter your search by size, file type or date modified. You can also see the latest searches that you have made.

How to Work with Libraries

Windows 8 has 4 main libraries: Documents, Music, Pictures and Videos. Whenever you need a specific file, you can search for them through the Libraries or groups of content that you can readily access via the File Explorer.

The folders and files that you create are not actually stored in the Libraries themselves. The libraries are just there to help you better organize your stuff. You can place your own folders inside the libraries without the need to change their actual location in your computer. For instance, you can place a folder your recent photos in the Pictures library and still keep the folder on your Desktop for ready access.

Libraries are particularly vital in Windows 8 since a lot of the applications on the Start screen such as Photos, Music and Vides use the libraries in looking for and displaying their content. For instance, all of the photos in your Pictures library are also in your Photos app.

You need to note that the applications on your Start screen are optimized for media so that it will be more trouble-free for you to watch videos, listen to music and view your pictures. The File Explorer is an essential tool in organizing your current media files into libraries so that you can easily enjoy them right from your Start screen.

The My Music, My Documents folders and other certain folders are automatically included in their own applicable libraries. But you can add your own folders to any of the Libraries by first locating the Folder you want to add and then right-clicking on it. Choose the Include in library and then choose your preferred library. This technique allows your folder to be both in your library and in its original location.

Chapter 5: How to Get Started with the Desktop

The Start screen really is a cool new feature of Windows 8. But if you will be doing more than surfing the internet, watching videos and listening to music, you need to familiarize yourself with the different features in the Desktop view.

How to Work with Files

The details of the File Explorer were already discussed in the previous chapter. In this chapter, you will learn how to open and delete files, navigate through the various folders, and more.

After you have opened the File Explorer and you instantly see the document that you wish to open, you can simply double-click on it to open it. But if you still need to go through the different folders, the Navigation pane is very useful in choosing a different folder or location.

How to Delete Files

You can delete a file by clicking, holding and dragging the file directly to the Recycle Bin icon found on the Desktop. An easier way is choosing the file that you want to delete and then pressing the Delete key. Do not worry if you have unintentionally deleted a file. You can access the Recycle Bin to locate the deleted file and restore it to its original folder. You can do this by right-clicking the file that you want to restore and then choosing Restore.

But if you are certain that all files in the Recycle Bin can be permanently deleted, you can clear it by right-clicking the Recycle Bin icon and then choosing Empty Recycle bin.

How to Open an Application on the Desktop

You can do this by either clicking the application icon found on the taskbar or double-clicking the application shortcut found on the Desktop.

How to Pin Applications to the Taskbar

By default, only selected application icons will be included on your taskbar. But you can pin your most used application on the taskbar so you can readily access them. You can do this by right-clicking anyplace on the Start screen. You will then see a menu at the bottom of your screen. Choose the All apps button to show the list of all your installed applications. Look for the application you want to pin and the right-click it and then choose Pin to taskbar. You need to note, though, that you cannot pin all applications to your taskbar. There are certain applications that are designed to be launched from the Start screen only like Calendar and Messaging. Thus, you can only pin them to the Start screen.

How to Use Desktop Effects

Multi-tasking and working with several windows have become easier with Windows 8 because of the various Desktop effects now available to you.

•   You can use the Snap effect to quickly resize open windows. This is particularly useful when you are working with several windows simultaneously. You can use the Snap effect by clicking, holding and dragging a window to the right or the left until you see the cursor reach the edge of your screen. Release your mouse to snap the window into place. You can easily unsnap a window by clicking, dragging it down and then releasing your mouse.

•   Use the Peek effect for viewing the open windows from your taskbar. You can do this by hovering your mouse over any app icon on the taskbar that you want to view. You will then see a thumbnail preview of all open windows. You can view the full-sized window of the application by hovering the mouse over the app in the thumbnail preview.

Programming Box Set #97: Windows 8 Tips for Beginners & PHP Programming Professional Made Easy

• Use the Shake feature for selecting a single window from a clutter of open windows and then minimizing the rest. You can do this by locating and selecting the window that you want to concentrate on. You can then gently shake the window back and forth to minimize the other open windows. When you shake the window once more, all of the windows that you minimized will get maximized again.

• The Flip feature is useful in scrolling across a preview of all your open windows. You can also view any of the open applications on your Start screen using the Flip preview. The first three features – Snap, Shake and Peek – are for use only on the Desktop view. The Flip feature, on the other hand, can be used similarly in both the Desktop view and the Start screen. You can access the Flip preview by pressing and holding the Alt key and then pressing the Tab key. While you are still pressing the Alt key, press the Tab key to continue scrolling through your open windows. When you have spotted the application or the window that you want to view, stop pressing the Alt and Tab keys to display the app or window.

Conclusion

Thank you again for purchasing this book!

I hope this book was able to help you to use the new features of Windows 8.

The next step is to start personalizing your own Windows 8 so you can get the most out of it.

Finally, if you enjoyed this book, please take the time to share your thoughts and post a review on Amazon. We do our best to reach out to readers and provide the best value we can. Your positive review will help us achieve that. It'd be greatly appreciated!

Thank you and good luck!

Book 2
PHP Programming
Professional Made Easy
BY SAM KEY

Expert PHP Programming Language Success in a Day for any Computer User!

Table of Contents

Introduction

I want to thank you and congratulate you for purchasing the book, "Professional PHP Programming Made Easy: Expert PHP Programming Language Success in a Day for any Computer User!"

This book contains proven steps and strategies on how to quickly transition from client side scripting to server side scripting using PHP.

The book contains a condensed version of all the topics you need to know about PHP as a beginner. To make it easier for you to understand the lessons, easy to do examples are included.

If you are familiar with programming, it will only take you an hour or two to master the basics of PHP. If you are new to programming, expect that you might take two to three days to get familiar with this great server scripting language.

Thanks again for purchasing this book, I hope you enjoy it!

Chapter 1: Setting Expectations and Preparation

PHP is a scripting language primarily used by web developers to create interactive and dynamic websites. This book will assume that you are already familiar with HTML and CSS. By the way, a little bit of XML experience is a plus.

This book will also assume that you have a good understanding and experience with JavaScript since most of the explanations and examples here will use references to that client side scripting language

To be honest, this will be like a reference book to PHP that contains bits of explanations. And since JavaScript is commonly treated as a prerequisite to learning PHP, it is expected that most web developers will experience no difficulty in shifting to using this server side scripting language.

However, if you have little knowledge of JavaScript or any other programming language, expect that you will have a steep learning curve if you use this book. Nevertheless, it does not mean that it is impossible to learn PHP without a solid background in programming or client side scripting. You just need to play more with the examples presented in this book to grasp the meaning and purpose of the lessons.

Anyway, unlike JavaScript or other programming languages, you cannot just test PHP codes in your computer. You will need a server to process it for you. There are three ways to do that:

1. Get a web hosting account. Most web hosting packages available on the web are PHP ready. All you need to do is code your script, save it as .php or .htm, upload it to your web directory, and access it.

2. Make your computer as simple web server. You can do that by installing a web server application in your computer. If your computer is running on Microsoft Windows, you can install XAMPP to make your computer act like a web server. Do not worry. Your computer will be safe since your XAMPP, by default, will make your computer only available to your use.

3. Use an online source code editor that can execute PHP codes. Take note that this will be a bit restricting since most of them only accept and execute PHP codes. It means that you will not be able to mix HTML, CSS, JavaScript, and PHP in one go. But if you are going to study the basics, which the lessons in this book are all about, it will be good enough.

Chapter 2: PHP Basics

This chapter will teach you the primary things that you need to know when starting to code PHP. It includes PHP's syntax rules, variables, constants, echo and print, operators, and superglobals.

Syntax

PHP code can be placed anywhere in an HTML document or it can be saved in a file with .php as its file extension. Just like JavaScript, you will need to enclose PHP code inside tags to separate it from HTML. The tag will tell browsers that all the lines inside it are PHP code.

PHP's opening tag is <?php and its closing tag is ?>. For example:

```
<!DOCTYPE html>
</html>
<head></head>
<body>
    <h1>Heading for the page</h2>
    <p>Some paragraph</p>
    <?php
        // Insert some PHP code in here.
    ?>
</body>
</html>
```

Echo and Print

PHP code blocks do not only return the values you requested from them, but you can also let it return HTML or text to the HTML file that invoked the PHP code blocks. To do that, you will need to use the echo or print command. Below are samples on how they can be used:

```
<?php
echo "Hello World!";
?>
<?php
print "Hello World!";
```

```
?>
```

Once the browser parses that part of the HTML, that small code will be processed on the server, and the server will send the value "Hello World" back to the client. Browsers handle echo and print values by placing them in the HTML file code. It will appear after the HTML element where the PHP code was inserted. For example:

```
<p>This is a paragraph.</p>
<?php
echo "Hello World!";
?>
<p>This is another paragraph.</p>
```

Once the browser parses those lines, this will be the result:

This is a paragraph.

Hello World!

This is another paragraph.

You can even echo HTML elements. For example:

```
<p>P1.</p>
<?php
print "<a href='http://www.google.com' >Google</a>";
?>
<p>P2.</p>
```

As you have witnessed, both echo and print have identical primary function, which is to send output to the browser. They have two differences however. Print can only handle one parameter while echo can handle multiple parameters. Another difference is that you can use print in expressions since it returns a value of 1 while you cannot use echo. Below is a demonstration of their differences:

```
<?php
echo "Hello World!", "How are you?";
?>
<?php
print "Hello World!", "How are you?";
?>
```

The echo code will be successfully sent to the client, but the print code will bring up a syntax error due to the unexpected comma (,) and the additional parameter or value after it. Though, if you want to use print with multiple parameters, you can concatenate the values of the parameters instead. String concatenation will be discussed later.

```php
<?php
$x = 1 + print("test");
echo $x;
?>
<?php
$x = 1 + echo("test");
echo $x;
?>
```

The variable $x will have a value of 2 since the expression print("test") will return a value of 1. Also, even it is used as a value in an expression, the print command will still produce an output.

On the other hand, the echo version of the code will return a syntax error due to the unexpected appearance of echo in the expression.

Many web developers use the echo and print commands to provide dynamic web content for small and simple projects. In advanced projects, using return to send an array of variables that contain HTML content and displaying them using JavaScript or any client side scripting is a much better method.

Variables

Creating a variable in JavaScript requires you to declare it and use the keyword var. In PHP, you do not need to declare to create a variable. All you need to do is assign a value in a variable for it to be created. Also, variables in PHP always starts with a dollar sign ($).

```php
<?php
$examplevariable = "Hello World!";
echo $examplevariable;
?>
```

There are rules to follow when creating a variable, which are similar to JavaScript's variable syntax.

➢ The variable's name or identifier must start with a dollar sign ($).

➢ An underscore or a letter must follow it.

> ➢ Placing a number or any symbol after the dollar sign instead will return a syntax error.

> ➢ The identifier must only contain letters, numbers, or underscores.

> ➢ Identifiers are case sensitive. The variable $x is treated differently from $X.

You can assign any type of data into a PHP variable. You can store strings, integers, floating numbers, and so on. If you have experienced coding using other programming languages, you might be thinking where you would need to declare the data type of the variable. You do not need to do that. PHP will handle that part for you. All you need to do is to assign the values in your variables.

Variable Scopes

Variables in PHP also change their scope, too, depending on the location where you created them.

Local

If you create a variable inside a function, it will be treated as a local variable. Unlike JavaScript, assigning a value to variable for the first time inside a function will not make them global due to way variables are created in PHP.

Global

If you want to create global variables, you can do it by creating a value outside your script's functions. Another method is to use the global keyword. The global keyword can let you create or access global variables inside a function. For example:

```php
<?php
function test() {
    global $x;
    $x = "Hello World!";
}
test();
echo $x;
?>
```

In the example above, the line global $x defined variable $x as a global variable. Because of that, the echo command outside the function was able to access $x without encountering an undefined variable error.

As mentioned a while ago, you can use the global keyword to access global variables inside functions. Below is an example:

```
<?php
$x = "Hello Word!";
function test() {
     global $x;
     echo $x;
}
test();
?>
```

Just like before, the command echo will not encounter an error as long as the global keyword was used for the variable $x.

Another method you can use is to access your script's global values array, $GLOBALS. With $GLOBALS, you can create or access global values. Here is the previous example used once again, but with the $GLOBALS array used instead of the global keyword:

```
<?php
function test() {
     $GLOBALS['x'] = "Hello World!";
}
test();
echo $x;
?>
```

Take note that when using $GLOBALS, you do not need the dollar sign when creating or accessing a variable.

Static

If you are not comfortable in using global variables just to keep the values that your functions use, you can opt to convert your local variables to static. Unlike local variables, static variables are not removed from the memory once the function that houses them ends. They will stay in the memory like global variables, but they will be only accessible on the functions they reside in. For example:

```
<?php
```

```
function test() {
      static $y = 1;
      if (empty($y))
            {$y = 1;}
      echo $y . " ";
      $y += $y;
}
test();
test();
test();
test();
test();
?>
```

In the example, the variable y's value is expected to grow double as the function is executed. With the help of static keyword, the existence and value of y is kept in the script even if the function where it serves as a local variable was already executed.

As you can see, together with the declaration that the variable y is static, the value of 1 was assigned to it. The assignment part in the declaration will only take effect during the first time the function was called and the static declaration was executed.

Superglobals

PHP has predefined global variables. They contain values that are commonly accessed, define, and manipulated in everyday server side data execution. Instead of manually capturing those values, PHP has placed them into its predefined superglobals to make the life of PHP programmers easier.

> - $GLOBALS

> - $_SERVER

> - $_REQUEST

> - $_POST

> - $_GET

> - $_FILES

> ➤ $_ENV

> ➤ $_COOKIE

> ➤ $_SESSION

Superglobals have CORE USES IN PHP SCRIPTING. YOU WILL BE MOSTLY USING ONLY FIVE OF THESE SUPERGLOBALS IN YOUR EARLY DAYS IN CODING PHP. THEY ARE: $GLOBALS, $_SERVER, $_REQUEST, $_POST, AND $_GET.

Constants

Constants are data storage containers just like variables, but they have global scope and can be assigned a value once. Also, the method of creating a constant is much different than creating a variable. When creating constants, you will need to use the define() construct. For example:

```php
<?php
define(this_is_a_constant, "the value", false);
?>
```

The define() construct has three parameters: define(name of constant, value of the constant, is case sensitive?). A valid constant name must start with a letter or an underscore – you do not need to place a dollar sign ($) before it. Aside from that, all other naming rules of variables apply to constants.

The third parameter requires a Boolean value. If the third parameter was given a true argument, constants can be accessed regardless of their case or capitalization. If set to false, its case will be strict. By default, it will be set to false.

Operators

By time, you must be already familiar with operators, so this book will only refresh you about them. Fortunately, the usage of operators in JavaScript and PHP is almost similar.

> ➤ Arithmetic: +, -, *, /, %, and **.

> ➤ Assignment: =, +=, -=, *=, /=, and %=.

> ➤ Comparison: ==, ===, !=, <>, !==, >, <, >=, and <=.

Programming Box Set #97: Windows 8 Tips for Beginners & PHP Programming Professional Made Easy

➢ Increment and Decrement: ++x, x++, --x, and x--.

➢ Logical: and, or, xor, &&, ||, and !.

➢ String: . and .=.

➢ Array: +, ==, ===, !=, <>, and !==.

Chapter 3: Flow Control

Flow control is needed when advancing or creating complex projects with any programming language. With them, you can control the blocks of statements that will be executed in your script or program. Most of the syntax and rules in the flow control constructs in PHP are almost similar to JavaScript, so you will not have a hard time learning to use them in your scripts.

Functions

Along the way, you will need to create functions for some of the frequently repeated procedures in your script. Creating functions in PHP is similar to JavaScript. The difference is that function names in PHP are not case sensitive. For example:

```php
<?php
function test($parameter = "no argument input") {
    print $parameter;
}
TEST("Success!");
tEsT();
?>
```

In JavaScript, calling a function using its name in different casing will cause an error. With PHP, you will encounter no problems or errors as long as the spelling of the name is correct.

Also, did you notice the variable assignment on the sample function's parameter? The value assigned to the parameter's purpose is to provide a default value to it when the function was called without any arguments being passed for the parameter.

In the example, the second invocation of the function test did not provide any arguments for the function to assign to the $parameter. Because of that, the value 'no argument input' was assigned to $parameter instead.

In JavaScript, providing a default value for a parameter without any value can be tricky and long depending on the number of parameters that will require default arguments or parameter values.

Of course, just like JavaScript, PHP functions also return values with the use of the return keyword.

If, Else, and Elseif Statements

PHP has the same if construct syntax as JavaScript. To create an if block, start by typing the if keyword, and then follow it with an expression to be evaluated inside parentheses. After that, place the statements for your if block inside curly braces. Below is an example:

```php
<?php
$color1 = "blue";
if ($color1 == "blue") {
        echo "The color is blue! Yay!";
}
?>
```

If you want your if statement to do something else if the condition returns a false, you can use else.

```php
<?php
$color1 = "blue";
if ($color1 == "blue") {
        echo "The color is blue! Yay!";
}
else {
        echo "The color is not blue, you liar!";
}
?>
```

In case you want to check for more conditions in your else statements, you can use elseif instead nesting an if statement inside else. For example:

```php
<?php
$color1 = "blue";
if ($color1 == "blue") {
        echo "The color is blue! Yay!";
}
else {
        if ($color == "green") {
                echo "Hmm. I like green, too. Yay!";
        }
        else {
```

```
        echo "The color is not blue, you liar!";
    }
}
?>
```
Is the same as:

```
<?php
$color1 = "blue";
if ($color1 == "blue") {
    echo "The color is blue! Yay!";
}
elseif ($color == "green" {
    echo "Hmm. I like green, too. Yay!";}
else {
    echo "The color is not blue, you liar!";
}
?>
```
Using elseif is less messy and is easier to read.

Switch Statement

However, if you are going to check for multiple conditions for one expression or variable and place a lot of statements per condition satisfied, it is better to use switch than if statements. For example, the previous if statement is the same as:

```
<?php
$color1 = "blue";
switch ($color1) {
    case "blue":
        echo "The color is blue! Yay!";
        break;
    case "green":
        echo "Hmm. I like green, too. Yay!";
        break;
    case default:
        echo "The color is not blue, you liar!";
}
?>
```
The keyword switch starts the switch statement. Besides it is the value or expression that you will test. It must be enclosed in parentheses.

Every case keyword entry must be accompanied with the value that you want to compare against the expression being tested. Each case statement can be translated as if <expression 1> is equal to <expression 2>, and then perform the statements below.

The break keyword is used to signal the script that the case block is over and the any following statements after it should not be done.

On the other hand, the default case will be executed when no case statements were satisfied by the expression being tested.

Chapter 4: Data Types – Part 1

PHP also has the same data types that you can create and use in other programming languages. Some of the data types in PHP have different ways of being created and assigned from the data types in JavaScript.

Strings

Any character or combination of characters placed in double or single quotes are considered strings in PHP. In PHP, you will deal with text a lot more often than other programming languages. PHP is used typically to handle data going from the client to the server and vice versa.   Due to that, you must familiarize yourself with a few of the most common used string operators and methods.

Numbers

Integer

Integers are whole numbers without fractional components or values after the decimal value. When assigning or using integers in PHP, it is important that you do not place blanks and commas between them to denote or separate place values.

An integer value can be positive, negative or zero. In PHP, you can display integers in three forms: decimal (base 10), octal (base 8), or hexadecimal (base 16). To denote that a value is in hexadecimal form, always put the prefix 0x (zero-x) with the value (e.g., 0x1F, 0x4E244D, 0xFF11AA). On the other hand, to denote that a value is in octal form, put the prefix 0 (zero) with the value (e.g., 045, 065, and 0254).

If you echo or print an integer variable, its value will be automatically presented in its decimal form. In case that you want to show it in hexadecimal or octal you can use dechex() or decoct() respectively. For example:

```
<?php
echo dechex(255);
echo decoct(9);
?>
```

The first echo will return FF, which is 255 in decimal. The second echo will return 11, which is 9 in octal. As you might have noticed, the prefix 0x and 0 were not present in the result. The prefixes only apply when you write those two presentations of integers in your script.

On the other hand, you can use hexdec() to reformat a hexadecimal value to decimal and use octdec() to reformat an octal value to decimal.

You might think of converting hex to oct or vice versa. Unfortunately, PHP does not have constructs like hexoct() or octhex(). To perform that kind of operation, you will need to manually convert the integer to decimal first then convert it to hex or oct.

Float or Double

Floating numbers are real numbers (or approximations of real numbers). In other words, it can contain fractional decimal values.

Since integers are a subset of real numbers, integers are floating numbers. Just adding a decimal point and a zero to an integer in PHP will make PHP consider that the type of the variable that will store that value is float instead of integer.

Boolean

Boolean is composed of two values: True and False. In PHP, true and false are not case sensitive. Both values are used primarily in conditional statements, just like in JavaScript.

Also, false is equivalent to null, a blank string, and 0 while true is equivalent to any number except 0 or any string that contains at least one character.

NULL

This is a special value type. In case that a variable does not contain a value from any other data types, it will have a NULL value instead. For example, if you try to access a property from an object that has not been assigned a value yet, it will have a NULL value. By the way, you can assign NULL to variables, too.

Resource

Resources is a special variable type. They only serve as a reference to external resource and are only created by special functions. An example of a resource is a database link.

Chapter 5: Data Types – Part 2

The data types explained in this chapter are essential to your PHP programming life. In other programming languages, you can live without this data types. However, in PHP, you will encounter them most of the time, especially if you will start to learn and use databases on your scripts.

ARRAYS

Arrays are data containers for multiple values. You can store numbers, strings, and even arrays in an array. Array in PHP is a tad different in JavaScript, so it will be discussed in detail in this book.

There are three types of array in PHP: indexed, associative, and multidimensional.

Indexed Arrays

Indexed array is the simplest form of arrays in PHP. For those people who are having a hard time understanding arrays, think of an array as a numbered list that starts with zero. To create or assign values to an array, you must use the construct array(). For example:

```
<?php
$examplearray = array(1, 2, "three");
?>
```

To call values inside an array, you must call them using their respective indices. For example:

```
<?php
$examplearray = array(1, 2, "three");
echo $examplearray[0];
echo $examplearray['2'];
?>
```

The first echo will reply with 1 and the second echo will reply three. As you can see, in indexed arrays, you can call values with just a number or a number inside quotes. When dealing with indexed arrays, it is best that you use the first method.

Since the number 1 was the first value to be assigned to the array, index 0 was assigned to it. The index number of the values in an array increment by 1. So, the index numbers of the values 2 and three are 1 and 2 respectively.

Associative Arrays

The biggest difference between associative arrays and indexed arrays is that you can define the index keys of the values in associative arrays. The variable $GLOBALS is one of the best example of associative arrays in PHP. To create an associative array, follow the example:

```php
<?php
$examplearray = array("index0" => "John", 2 => "Marci");
echo $examplearray["index0"];
echo $examplearray[2];
?>
```

The first echo will return John and the second echo will return Marci. Take note that if you use associative array, the values will not have indexed numbers.

Multidimensional Arrays

Multidimensional arrays can store values, indexed arrays, and associative arrays. If you create an array in your script, the $GLOBALS variable will become a multidimensional array. You can insert indexed or associative arrays in multidimensional arrays. However, take note that the same rules apply to their index keys. To create one, follow the example below:

```php
<?php
$examplearray = array(array("test1", 1, 2), array("test2" => 3, "test3" => 4), array("test4", 5, 6));
echo $examplearray[1]["test2"];
echo $examplearray[1][1];
echo $examplearray[2][0];
?>
```

As you can see, creating multidimensional arrays is just like nesting arrays on its value. Calling values from multidimensional is simple.

If a value was assigned, it can be called like a regular array value using its index key. If a value was paired with a named key, it can be called by its name. If an array was assigned, you can call the value inside it by calling the index key of the array first, and then the index key of the value inside it.

In the example, the third echo called the array in index 2 and accessed the value located on its 0 index. Hence, it returned test4.

Objects

Objects are like small programs inside your script. You can assign variables within them called properties. You can also assign functions within them called methods.

Creating and using objects can make you save hundreds of lines of code, especially if you have some bundle of codes that you need to use repeatedly on your scripts. To be on the safe side, the advantages of using objects depend on the situation and your preferences.

Debates about using objects in their scripts (object oriented programming) or using functions (procedural programming) instead have been going on forever. It is up to you if you will revolve your programs around objects or not.

Nevertheless, to create objects, you must create a class for them first. Below is an example on how to create a class in PHP.

```php
<?php
class Posts {
        function getPost() {
                $this->post1 = "Post Number 1.";
        }
        var $post2 = "Post Number 2.";
}

$test = new Posts();
echo $test->post2;
$test->getPost();
echo $test->post1;
?>
```

In this example, a new class was created using the class keyword. The name of the class being created is Posts. In class declarations, you can create functions that will be methods for the objects under the class. And you can create variables that will be properties for the subjects under the class.

First, a function was declared. If the function was called, it will create a property for an object under the Posts class called post1. Also, a value was assigned to it. You might have noticed the $this part in the declaration inside the function. The $this variable represents the object that owns the function being declared.

Besides it is a dash and a chevron (->). Some programmers informally call it as the instance operator. This operator allows access to the instances (methods and properties) of an object. In the statement, the script is accessing the post1 property inside the $this object, which is the object that owns the function. After accessing the property, the statement assigned a value to it.

Aside from the function or method declaration, the script created a property called post2, which is a variable owned by the Posts class. To declare one, you need to use the keyword var (much like in JavaScript). After this statement, the class declaration ends.

The next statement contains the variable assignment, $test = new Posts(). Technically, that means that the variable $test will become a new object under the Posts class. All the methods and properties that was declared inside the Posts() class declaration will be given to it.

To test if the $test class became a container for a Posts object, the script accessed the property post2 from $test and then echoed it to produce an output. The echo will return , 'Post number 2.'. Indeed, the $test variable is already an object under the Posts class.

What if you call and print the property post1 from the variable $test? It will not return anything since it has not been created or initialized yet. To make it available, you need to invoke the getPost() method of $test. Once you do, you will be able to access the property post1.

And that is just the tip of the iceberg. You will be working more on objects on advanced PHP projects.

Conclusion

Thank you again for purchasing this book!

I hope this book was able to help you to learn PHP fast.

The next step is to:

Learn the other superglobals

Learn from handling in HTML, JavaScript, and PHP

Learn using MySQL

Finally, if you enjoyed this book, please take the time to share your thoughts and post a review on Amazon. We do our best to reach out to readers and provide the best value we can. Your positive review will help us achieve that. It'd be greatly appreciated!

Thank you and good luck!

Check Out My Other Books

Below you'll find some of my other popular books that are popular on Amazon and Kindle as well. Simply click on the links below to check them out. Alternatively, you can visit my author page on Amazon to see other work done by me.

Android Programming in a Day

Python Programming in a Day

C Programming Success in a Day

CSS Programming Professional Made Easy

C Programming Professional Made Easy

JavaScript Programming Made Easy

Windows 8 Tips for Beginners

Windows 8 Tips for Beginners

HTML Professional Programming Made Easy

Programming Box Set #97: Windows 8 Tips for Beginners & PHP Programming Professional Made Easy

C ++ Programming Success in a Day

If the links do not work, for whatever reason, you can simply search for these titles on the Amazon website to find them.

www.ingramcontent.com/pod-product-compliance
Lightning Source LLC
Chambersburg PA
CBHW060928050326
40689CB00013B/3006